# Balloon
## F·U·N

## Nick Huckleberry Beak

LORENZ BOOKS
NEW YORK · LONDON · SYDNEY · BATH

This edition published in 1996 by Lorenz Books
an imprint of Anness Publishing Limited,
administrative office: 27 West 20th Street
New York, NY 10011

Lorenz Books are available for bulk purchase and for premium use.
For details write or call the manager of special sales,
LORENZ BOOKS, 27 West 20th Street, New York, NY 10011; (212) 807-6739

ISBN 1 85967 319 8

*Publisher:* Joanna Lorenz
*Senior Children's Editor:* Sue Grabham
*Editor:* Sophie Warne
*Photographer:* John Freeman
*Designer:* Edward Kinsey

Printed in China

# Introduction

Twist, twist, bend, bend, stretch, twist and pop! No, it's not a new dance, nor a new breakfast cereal – it's you, after you've read this book and caught the balloon modeling bug. Yes, we're going to create a world of hairless dogs, furless rabbits, banana-less monkeys and silly swans.

Confused? Well, you won't be for much longer. Grab a bag of balloons and let your imagination take over. First you'll start making models for fun, then for friends and at parties. Finally you'll be making them at school, for your little brother or sister, or even for an audience! Before you know it you won't have gone crazy, you'll have become ... a balloonatic!

Well, what are you waiting for – turn the page!

Nick Huckleberry Beak

# Contents

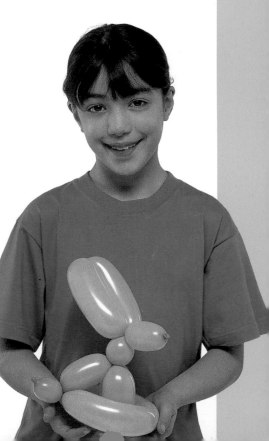

# Safety and Equipment

Although you can have a lot of fun with these balloons, they can be dangerous, so please follow a few simple precautions:

**1** Always keep uninflated or burst balloons away from young children and animals to prevent choking accidents.

**2** Never put a balloon in your mouth.

**3** Keep balloons away from your eyes, especially when stretching or inflating them.

**4** Always use a balloon pump. Modeling balloons are very difficult to inflate and can cause damage to the lungs or ears if you try to inflate them without a pump.

**BALLOONS**

All the balloon projects in this book are made from "260"-type modeling balloons. These come in a variety of colors, usually in bags of 100. Some hobby and toy stores sell bags of single colors and larger quantities. Balloons are best used soon after purchasing and are best stored at room temperature in a dark place.

## PUMPS

There are many types of suitable pumps available, but don't get them confused with a normal balloon pump. You need a pump with a tapered nozzle on the end. The best are double-action pumps, which inflate the balloon when you push the pump in and when you pull it out. Try a few,

and see which one you prefer.

## PENS

Sometimes it's fun to draw faces or designs on your balloon model to bring it to life. Dry-wipe board markers are pretty good, as are some of the permanent ink pens that are available. It's a good idea to take a balloon with you when you go to buy a new pen, so you can test it out and see how well it performs.

7

# Inflating Balloons and Tying Knots

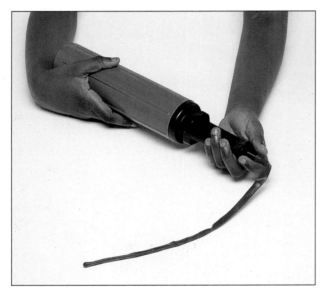

**1** Modeling balloons are easier to inflate and less likely to burst if they are warm. You can warm them by stretching them a few times and by keeping them out of the fridge! Insert the nozzle of the pump into the mouth of the balloon. Hold the balloon on the nozzle.

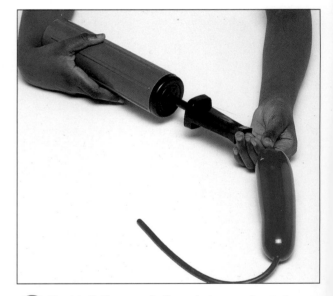

**2** Start inflating your balloon, but remember to leave an uninflated bit at the end. This is important, as each time you twist the inflated balloon a little air moves into this end portion. Usually, the more twists a model contains, the longer the uninflated end should be.

## HANDY HINT

*Bang! Yes, some balloons are (pop! burst!) weaker than others. On average, about one in every 25–30 balloons bursts during inflating, so don't (bang!) worry – it's not your fault.*

**3** The knot is often the cause of much frustration, but it's not that difficult to tie. Stretch the end of the balloon around two fingers (ouch!), but not too tightly.

**4** Continue pulling the end of the balloon until it overlaps to form a complete circle around both fingers. Use your thumb to hold in place.

**5** Tuck the end of the balloon down between the two fingers and through the circle – in other words, tie the knot!

**6** Keeping hold of the end, slip your fingers out of the knot and pull it tight. That wasn't too difficult, was it?

**TIP**

*If you're still having trouble, don't give up! You'll just have to practice more, or invent an automatic balloon-tying machine!*

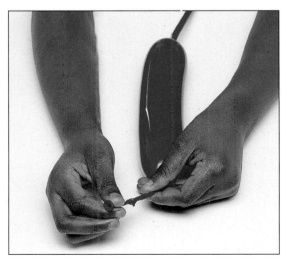

# Basic Twists

Although the pictures and instructions for each balloon project are fairly easy to follow, here are a few of the basic twists that you will be using.

## LOCK TWIST

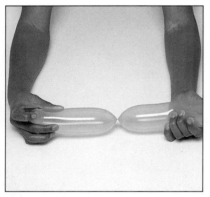 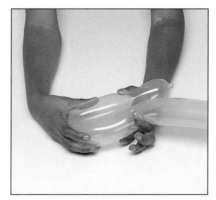 

**1** Here is a simple twist. If you stretch the balloon a little while twisting, it keeps the balloon from rubbing on itself and makes it less likely to burst. Keep hold of the balloon, as it will untwist if you let go.

**2** To prevent the balloon from untwisting, secure it with a lock twist. Fold the twisted balloon over, and pinch between finger and thumb.

**3** Twist the balloon below the finger and thumb to lock the two bubbles into place. You can let go now – the twist should stay in place.

## INTERLOCKING TWIST

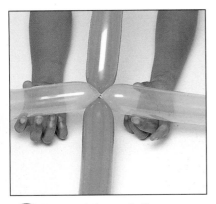
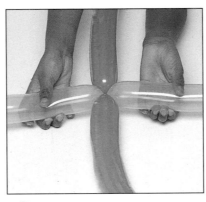

**1** You can join two balloons together with an interlocking twist. First, make a single twist in each balloon. Then, place one balloon over the other to make a cross.

**2** Twist one balloon around the other to join them together. This twist is useful when making intricate hats.

## LOOP TWIST

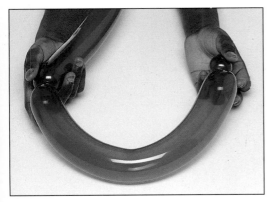

**1** The loop twist will really send you around the bend. Make two twists in a balloon to give you a twist at each end of a long bubble.

**2** Wrap one end of the balloon around the other to lock the twists together. You can make a large or small loop. This twist is ideal for the ears or legs of an animal.

# More Twists

## PINCH TWIST

**1** When a loop twist becomes so small that the bubble formed bends in on itself, it is called a pinch twist. This is because you pinch the bubble before twisting. This one is difficult, so be patient.

**2** Isn't it cute? The pinch twist is good for making ears and noses, and it's the only twist used in making the caterpillar model.

## TULIP TWIST

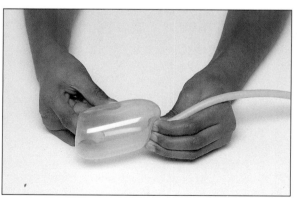

**1** Inflate a balloon, leaving a bit uninflated at the end. Push the knot into the balloon with your finger.

**2** Take hold of the knot from outside the balloon and remove your finger. Keeping hold of the knot, twist the balloon around several times to hold the knot in place.

# Balloon Decorations

You can make your balloon model more colorful, realistic or comical by using felt tip markers.

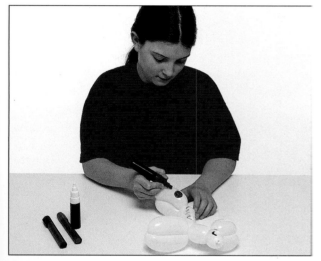

**1** The simplest and quickest way to decorate balloons is to use markers. As well as a variety of bright colors, get hold of a white paint pen if possible. White is really effective when drawing eyes, as it makes them stand out from the background.

**2** Eyes, a nose and a mouth are probably the first things you'll want to give your balloon model. Why not also try paws, hands or feet, feathers or fur, or just wild and wonderful patterns? You can also stick paper or material onto your balloon with tape, but be careful, as moving the tape will burst the balloon.

**TIP**
*It's a good idea to sketch your designs on paper first. You won't be able to rub them off once they are on the balloon.*

13

# Your First Animal

Here we go with your first balloon model. This one should look like a dog, but don't worry if your first attempt looks more like a bunch of grapes – keep trying! Remember, the size of your dog depends on how much you have inflated the balloon. Your end model could look like anything from a sausage dog to a poodle!

**TIP**

*Once you've made your first model, try making more with differently sized ears, bodies and legs. It's good practice for later models, and you may end up inventing an animal all your own.*

**1** Are you ready? Inflate your balloon, leaving 9 in uninflated at the end. Now twist three bubbles 3 in in length and hold onto them.

**2** To form the ears, twist the second and third bubbles together. They should now be locked in place, even when you let go. This is the dog's head.

**3** The front legs are made by twisting two slightly larger bubbles together and locking them in position. Remember to leave a gap for the dog's neck.

**4** Finally, leave a portion of balloon for the body, and twist together two bubbles to make the back legs. Now you've finished – good job! Does your dog look anything like this one?

# Ears and Noses

Ears and noses can really change the character of a balloon model. Experiment with different sizes to produce your desired effect.

**1** To make a small nose, twist a small bubble at the knotted end of the balloon. Don't let go yet!

② Pull the knotted end of the balloon down towards the twisted end of the bubble and twist it so that it locks in place.

③ You should now have a finished nose. You can make it bigger or smaller, depending on the animal.

④ To make the first ear, twist a bubble 3½–4½ in in length.

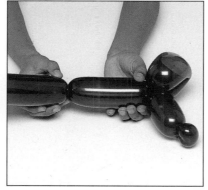

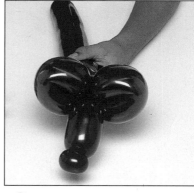

⑤ Squeeze this bubble to make a loop. Twist the ends together to lock it in position.

⑥ Twist another bubble 3½–4½in long for the second ear. Squeeze the bubble and twist the ends together as before.

⑦ As you can see, these looped ears look great and give your animal a dramatically different appearance. The same loop twists can be used to make legs.

# Mouse

The mouse is one of my favorites – it's just so cute! Why not make a whole family of different colored balloon mice?

**1** For a little mouse you need a little balloon, so inflate only a third of the balloon to leave a long uninflated tail.

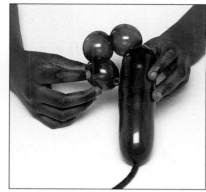

**2** To form the head, twist three small bubbles each approximately 1 in long. Twist and lock the second and third bubbles together to make the ears.

**3** Again, twist three small bubbles of the same size to make the neck and front legs. Twist and lock the second and third bubbles as before. This is getting easy, huh?

**4** Can you guess what comes next? You've got it – another three bubbles! Twist and lock these to make the body and back legs. The rest of the balloon is the mouse's long tail.

# Giraffe

Now we are looking up in the world! Someone once said that giraffes have such long necks so that they won't have to smell their own feet. Do you think that's true?

**HANDY HINT**
*Keep the body of the giraffe short, as this will make the neck look longer.*

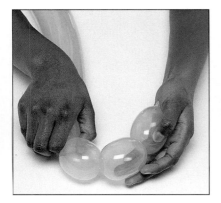

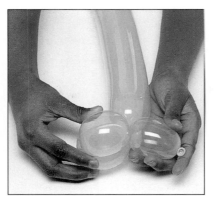

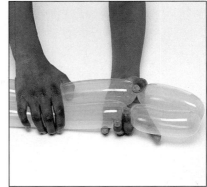

**1** Your balloon needs a 3 in uninflated end this time. As in the previous projects, you should form the head of the animal first. Prepare three bubbles 2 in long.

**2** Twist and lock the second and third bubbles together to form the ears. I bet this twisting business is getting easier by now!

**3** Leave a long portion of the balloon for the giraffe's neck, and twist two bubbles to make the front legs. The legs should be approximately 3–4 in long so that your giraffe is in proportion.

**4** Finally, twist two bubbles together for the back legs, leaving a short tail.

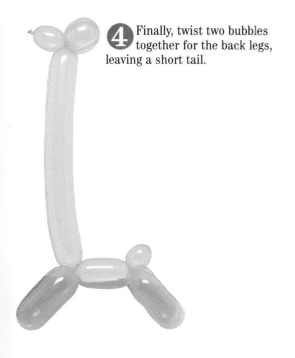

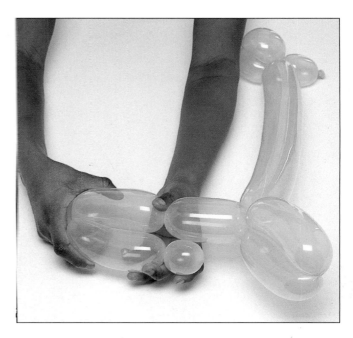

**21**

# Sitting Rabbit

Why not make your rabbit more lifelike by drawing on teeth and eyes? You could even make a running rabbit with two long jumping back legs instead of a sitting rabbit with looped legs.

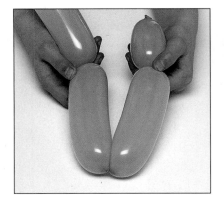

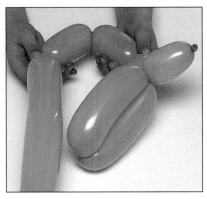

**1** Make a small bubble for the rabbit's head. Then make two longer bubbles, approximately 4 in each, for the ears.

**2** Twist the two long bubbles together. Leave a small gap for the neck, then twist two bubbles 3 in long for the front legs.

**3** Does it look good so far? This time the back legs are formed as a big loop. You'll see why later. First, twist a long bubble, leaving a small bubble at the end of the balloon. Loop the long bubble, and twist the ends together.

**4** Tuck the short front legs into the looped back legs. Your rabbit should now sit by itself quite happily.

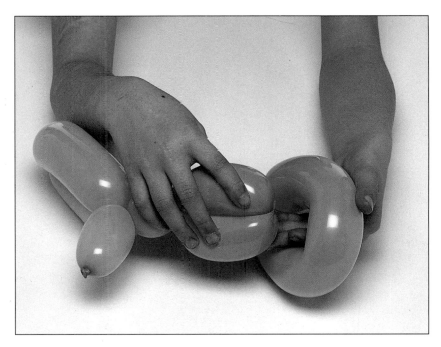

# Parrot on a Perch

Pretty Polly! This parrot is really popular, and you can see why. It can even be worn as a very unusual hat if you place the loop of the perch around your head!

**1** The parrot is a little different from the other balloon animals, so it may take more practice to perfect. Start by making a small bubble at the knotted end of the balloon for the parrot's beak.

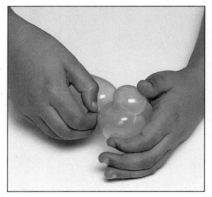

**2** Pull the knot and bubble down beside the rest of the balloon. Twist the knot around the balloon to form another bubble. The first small bubble is now stretched and should look like a beak on the head of the parrot.

**3** You'll wonder why you're making the next move, but don't worry, it should be fine! Form a large loop. Twist and lock it below the head, leaving a tail end of 7–8 in.

**4** This is the hard part, so good luck! Position the tail in the middle of the loop. Pinch and twist the tail and the two sides of the loop together, approximately 3 in below the head, to make the parrot's body and wings. All you need to do now is arrange the parrot on its perch.

## HANDY HINT

*This parrot on a perch makes a great decoration. Simply tie one end of a piece of string around the top of the perch and attach the other end to your bedroom wall or ceiling.*

# Bunch of Tulips

What a beautiful bouquet! These balloon flowers last longer than real tulips and they don't need water! You could tie a big, colorful ribbon around the stems to make a one-of-a-kind present.

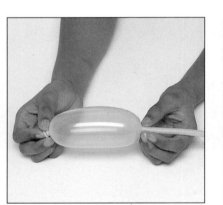

**1** Inflate only 3 in of the balloon, leaving a very long end for the stem. Now hold the two ends of the inflated section of the balloon, with one finger on the knot.

**2** Use your finger to push the knot into the balloon. This will take a bit of practice, so don't give up after your first time.

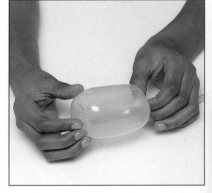

**3** Take hold of the knot with your other hand, and remove your finger. Holding the knot, twist the balloon around several times to hold the knot in place. There should now be a thin stripe down the center of the balloon.

**4** Well, that was more complicated to explain than to make, wasn't it? Go on, make some more in different colors, and give them to a friend.

# Sword

What kind of sword can't even cut through butter? You're about to make one! Well, at least you won't hurt anyone. Why not twist a balloon around your waist to make a belt for holding your sword? You could probably even make a shield, but don't ask me how because I've never tried!

**1** Inflate your balloon, leaving a 2 in uninflated end. Use the tulip twist to make the base of the handle. Push the knot into the balloon. With your other hand around the balloon, take hold of the knot and twist to hold it in place.

**2** Now make the protective part of the handle. You will need three loops. First, loop the balloon and pinch to form a loop above the base of the handle.

**3** Twist and lock the loop into place. Now form a second loop the same size as the first. Try to keep these loops fairly small so that your sword will be long.

28

**4** Twist and lock the second loop. Now form a third and final loop. You'll be good at making loops by the time you've finished this!

**TIP**

*Remember that balloon swords burst easily, so handle them with care.*

# Elephant

Here is a little elephant
with a great big nose. If
you want, you can make
the ears bigger and the
trunk shorter – it will
look just as funny!

**1** This model is also a little different from the other balloon animals because you start with the tail and work up towards the head. Inflate your balloon, leaving a 3 in uninflated end. Make one small bubble 1 in long and two slightly larger ones 1½ in long.

**2** Twist and lock the two larger bubbles to form the back legs. The smaller bubble is for the tail. Make three more bubbles for the body and front legs.

**3** Twist and lock the front legs into position. Now form a small bubble for the neck and a long bubble of 4 in or more for the first ear. Loop twist the longer bubble in place.

**4** Make another 4 in bubble and loop twist it in place for the second ear. Now slightly bend the rest of the balloon to make a curved trunk.

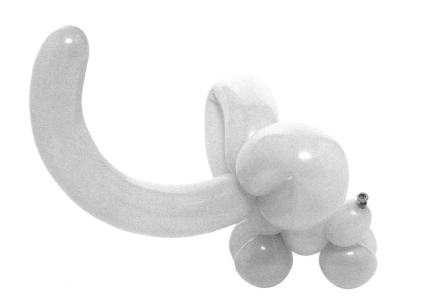

# Swan

Aren't they beautiful? Get rid of your rubber ducky and put one of these in your tub instead – they really do swim well!

**1** This is a beautiful balloon model that is easy to make. Inflate your balloon, leaving only a very short uninflated end. Make two large bubbles 11 in long.

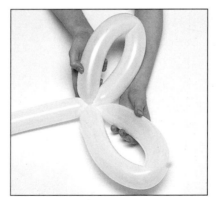

**2** Loop both of the large bubbles and twist the ends together. You should now have two large loops and a straight portion of balloon.

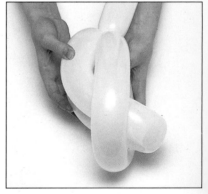

**3** Tuck one loop inside the other. Arrange the loops carefully to make the swan's body with the wings sticking up at the top.

**4** To create the elegant curved neck of the swan, pinch the end of the balloon and bend it around.

### HANDY HINT

*Balloon swans are great for floating in the bath or swimming pool, but remember they burst easily!*

33

# Caterpillar

This friendly caterpillar can
be made to stand upright
or creep along the floor.
It helps to add some
eyes so that you
know which
end is which!

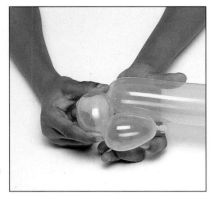

**1** Inflate a balloon, leaving a 5 in uninflated end. Twist a 1½ in bubble and then a 1 in bubble. Hold the bubbles firmly.

**2** Now pinch and twist the second bubble. It's not easy, but keep practicing because it's the only twist you will make for this caterpillar model.

**3** Now prepare another 1 in bubble to be pinch twisted. You'll be an expert at this twist soon!

**4** Now make another two 1 in bubbles and pinch twist the second one.

**5** Make another bubble and, yes, pinch twist it!

**6** Continue making two small bubbles and pinch twisting one of them until you reach the end of the balloon.

# Monkey Up a Tree

Here's your monkey up a tree with its long arms wrapped around the trunk. Where do you think the tree came from? It looks a lot like the balloon sword.... See if you can figure it out yourself.

**1** Inflate a balloon, leaving a 4 in uninflated end. Make one bubble 5 cm long and three more 1 in long. Now twist the end of the first bubble with the end of the last bubble, leaving the larger bubble sticking out from a loop of three smaller bubbles. Confused? Just be glad you don't have to explain this!

**2** Now twist the second and fourth bubbles in a pinch twist. This is the same as forming a loop, except that because the bubble is so small, you have to pinch it to twist its ends together.

**3** Here you can see the final pinch twist to make the ears. Does your monkey look anything like this one? Don't worry if you found this hard – it will get easier with practice.

36

**4** Make a small bubble for the neck, and then twist and lock a large loop for the front legs.

**5** Twist three more bubbles for the body and smaller back legs. You should be left with a long tail.

# Sunflower

Go on, make a few of these sunflowers and, together with some balloon tulips, you could make a terrific gift for a friend.

**TIP**

*If you keep these sunflowers in a vase, don't add water – they don't seem to need it!*

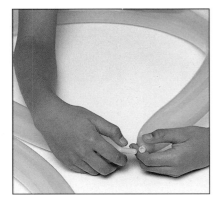

**1** Inflate two balloons, leaving only a very short uninflated end in each one. Tie the ends together so you are left with two large circles.

**2** Now twist each loop in the middle to make the shape of a number eight. You should find this part easy.

**3** Twist the two shapes together in the middle to make a cross. These are the petals.

**4** Inflate another balloon, once again leaving only a small uninflated end. Twist a loop in the center of the balloon. Twist another loop next to the first one. You should now have your stem and two leaves.

**5** Finally, insert the end of the stem balloon into the petals and twist it to lock it in place.

# Big Fish

Sure, this is a big fish, but it looks like a vegetarian, so you should be safe. This fish has an eye, but you could draw on scales or colored markings. Some tropical fish are really unusual looking!

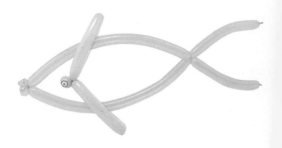

**1** Almost fully inflate two balloons. Make a small bubble in the end of each balloon using the tulip twist. You must be good at this by now. No? Better keep practicing!

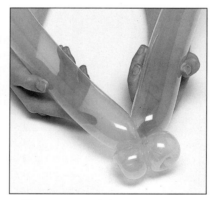

**2** Carefully twist the two balloons together at the base of the tulip twists. These two bubbles form the mouth of your fish.

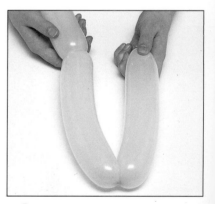

**3** Inflate another balloon, preferably in another color, leaving a short uninflated end. Make two long bubbles and twist the ends together. This should use up just under half the length of the balloon.

**4** Now make a small bubble, approximately 2 in long, in the center of the balloon. Pinch twist the bubble into place to make an eye.

**5** Once again, form two long bubbles and twist the ends together. You now have the fins and have done most of the hard work.

**6** Slide the fins into the first two joined balloons. Do this carefully because the balloons might burst if they rub together.

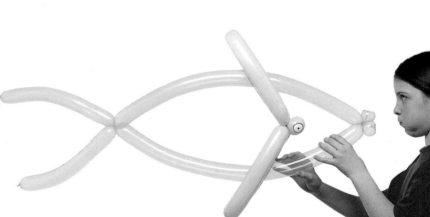

**7** Now interlock the ends of the balloons to form the tail. That wasn't too hard, was it?

# Acrobatic Airplane

Although this is a good model, you probably wouldn't want to go flying in it. Just imagine opening the door – all the air would rush out! Try hanging your plane from the ceiling with a piece of string, or make a mobile. Whatever you do, happy landing!

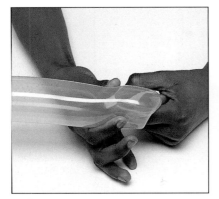 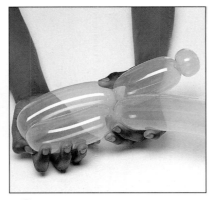 

**1** Inflate your balloon, leaving a 2 in uninflated end. Use the tulip twist to make a small bubble. This is the propellor, so try to keep it small and flat so it will be more realistic.

**2** Make a 2 in bubble and two 4½ in bubbles. Twist the longer two bubbles together to make one wing.

**3** Make two more 4½ in bubbles for the second wing. You're almost ready for take-off!

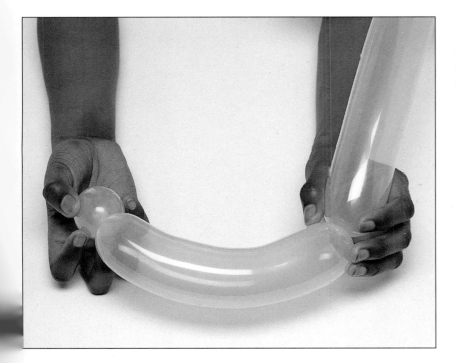

**4** At the tail end of the balloon, twist a 1 in bubble and a 4½ in bubble. Twist the larger one into a loop to make the tail of the plane.

# Reindeer

Not a sleigh in sight, yet here's a reindeer! At Christmas time, why not draw on a red nose and call him Rudolph?

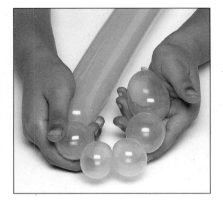

**1** You're going to have your hands full of bubbles with this model, but it's not too hard. Inflate your balloon, leaving a 3½ in uninflated end. Make a 1½–2 in bubble followed by four 1 in bubbles.

**2** Twist the base of the first and fourth small bubbles together to form a square of bubbles. This is one half of the deer's antlers. Now form four more 1 in bubbles.

**3** Twist the second set of bubbles to complete the antlers. Make and twist the front legs. (You should know how to do this by now!)

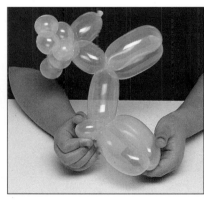

**4** Complete the back legs and tail, and you've done it! As you can see, the reindeer is very similar to the dog, except that now the ears are antlers.

**TIP**

*Here we used only four bubbles per antler, but you could increase this to six, or even eight bubbles. It's good practice, but remember to leave a longer uninflated end to start with.*

# Teddy Bear

Well, you can see what's happening here – the bear doesn't want to sit on its own. It's much happier climbing up your arm! You could also make a teddy bear hat for an unusual look.

**1** There are lots of twists here, so leave a 4 in uninflated end in your balloon. Make a 2 in bubble and a 1 in bubble, then a 1½ in bubble, three 1 in bubbles and another 1½ in bubble.

**2** To make the bear's face, follow the picture above carefully. Twist the two 1½ in bubbles together to form a circle of bubbles. Push the first bubble into the center of the circle of bubbles so that it sticks out on the other side.

**3** Pinch twist one of the 1 in bubbles to make the first ear. Now do the same for the second ear, and the hard part's over now – good job!

**4** Leave a small bubble for the neck, then twist two longer bubbles for the front paws. Now you could make just the two back legs and finish your bear, but try the following steps instead.

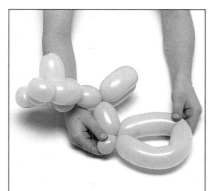

**5** Make a long bubble and loop twist it, leaving a small bubble for the tail.

**6** Just like with the balloon rabbit, if you push the front paws into the looped legs, your teddy bear will sit by itself quite happily.

# Your Own Pair of Ears?

With a little lump of cheese and these goofy balloon ears, you can transform yourself into a rabbit or a mouse! Squeak, squeak!

**1** Inflate two balloons, leaving only a small uninflated end in each. Twist each balloon in the middle and tie its ends together. These are going to be your new ears – I bet you can't wait!

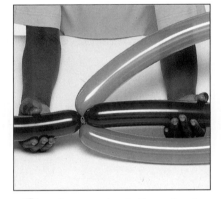

**2** Inflate another balloon, leaving only a small uninflated end. Tie on one of the ears, about 4 in from the middle of this balloon, using an interlocking twist.

**3** Twist on the other ear, about 4 in from the center, on the other side. Depending on the size of your head, you may have to move the ears around a little.

**4** Secure the ears around your
head with an interlocking
twist. They can be easily adjusted
to fit anyone.

49

# Dog on a Hat

You don't need a leash for this little dog – he'll just hold on tight and watch the world go by.

**TIP**

*Why not make other balloon animals to sit on top of your hat? You can do this just by changing their legs to loops. Monkey hats, teddy bear hats, giraffe hats are all possible and equally fun!*

50

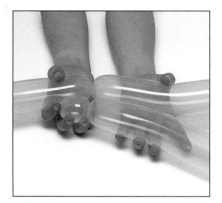

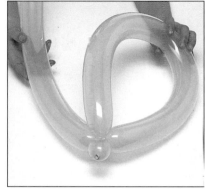

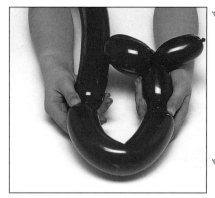

**1** The size of the hat will depend on the size of your head. Inflate your balloon, leaving only a small uninflated end. Twist a 1 in bubble, followed by a bubble long enough to fit around your head.

**2** Twist the ends of the bubbles together to make the headband part of the hat. Now inflate another balloon and start to make a dog.

**3** Make a dog the same way you did before, but use loops for the front and back legs.

**4** Push the free end of your headband balloon through the looped legs of the dog, and slide the dog along. Now you know why this dog has looped legs!

**5** Make a small bubble at the very end of the balloon. Twist and lock this bubble onto the headband opposite the first twist.

**51**

# Twirly Hat

You'll get plenty of great compliments when you wear this hat to your next party. Twirl away!

**TIP**

*This hat looks good when you use two different colored balloons, but even better with three or four! If you attach two more balloons to the headband, you can then twist all four balloons together.*

52

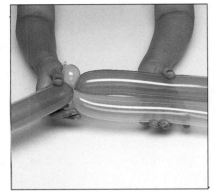

**1** Fully inflate two balloons. Make a small bubble in one balloon. Twist this onto the second balloon 6–8 in from the end, depending on your head size.

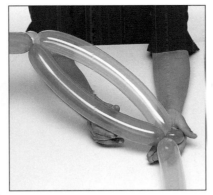

**2** Now form a small bubble in the second balloon and twist it onto the first balloon to complete the headband. After making a few of these, you'll automatically know when the headband is the right size.

**3** Now for the fun part! Slowly start twisting the balloons around each other to make a spiral.

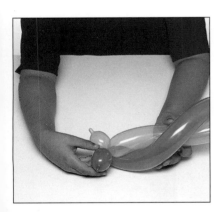

**4** At the top, pinch both balloons, twisting and locking them into position so that they don't uncurl.

# King of Hearts

This elegant crown will make you look like the King or Queen of Hearts. You don't have to add a balloon to the top of your hat, but why not? You could add a round balloon, a twirly balloon, even some bits of ribbon. Go on, have some fun!

**HANDY HINT**
*Why not make balloon hats with your friends to see who has the most imaginative and fun ideas?*

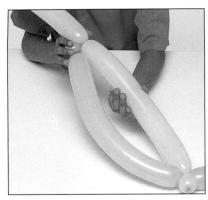

**1** Fully inflate two balloons and twist them together to make a headband. Try to make sure that the ends sticking out from the headband are the same length.

**2** Interlock and twist the two free ends, just under halfway down their length.

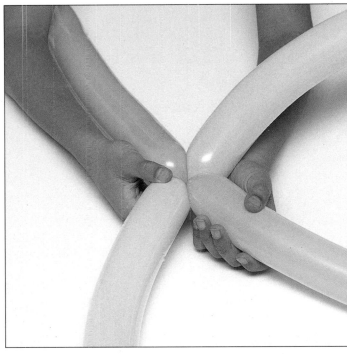

**3** Make a small bubble in the end of one free end. Twist it onto the headband halfway along one side.

**4** Twist the other free end onto the other side of the headband in the same way. You're just about ready for the coronation! Attach a balloon to the top of your crown for decoration if you want to.

55

# Build Your Own House

This house looks impressive when finished, and it's really fun to build. Use your imagination to add extra rooms or make balloon doors, windows, trees and lamp-posts. Make it as big as you like, but remember that it won't be warm in winter and you'll get soaked when it rains!

**1** Fully inflate 17 balloons – this is a big model! First, twist the ends together to make two squares. That used up eight of your balloons – only nine to go!

**2** Use four more balloons to link the two squares together and make a cube. Twist the ends to hold it together.

**3** Attach a balloon to each top corner of the cube. Twist these balloons together to make two triangles. Add a final balloon between the two triangles to finish the house.

**4** Well done! Once you get this far, you could add extra rooms, or make balloon windows and doors.

**5** Why not see what other buildings or shelters you can make? Here is a lopsided teepee! Can you make one?

**TIP**

*The house here is multi-colored, but your house could have walls made from red balloons and a roof made from black balloons.*

57

# Ball in the Balloon

What's this? A transparent dog? We can see what it's eaten for breakfast, or did it just swallow a ball? You'll probably pop lots of balloons perfecting this model – it's a tough one to master.

**HANDY HINT**

*Clear balloons can be hard to find. Don't worry if you can't find any – yellow balloons work just as well. You can, of course, put a bubble inside any colored balloon – it just means the ball won't be easy to see unless you hold the model up to the light.*

**1** Inflate your balloon, leaving a small uninflated end. Make a small bubble at the end. The bubble should be smaller than the width of the balloon.

**2** With your finger, carefully but firmly push the small bubble into the balloon. Hold onto the balloon firmly with your other hand or it will shoot off.

**3** With your free hand, pinch the bubble from the outside of the balloon to hold it in place. Remove your finger and grasp the very end of the balloon.

**4** Now you have to snap the thin rubber strand attaching the bubble to the end of the balloon. Do this by pulling your hands sharply apart. You may have to do it several times.

**5** The bubble should now be free inside the balloon. Carefully tie a knot in the new end of the balloon and then you can let go. Make your favorite model, and watch the ball rolling around inside it.

# Crazy Balloon Tricks

Impress your friends with these tricky balloon stunts, but don't give your secrets away!

**1** To prepare for the first trick, inflate a balloon, leaving a long uninflated end. Pinch the very end of the uninflated part of the balloon with both hands. Now stretch this a few times – go on, really pull.

**2** To perform the trick, twist a bubble 3 in long at the end of the balloon and hold it in your hand. When you squeeze the bubble, can you guess what will happen?

**3** Squeeze the bubble hard. You should get another bubble at the end of the tail. If not, stretch the balloon some more and try squeezing again.

**1** For your next trick, take two uninflated balloons of the same color. Cut the end off one of them using a pair of scissors. Slip the cut-off end onto the end of the whole balloon, and you are ready.

**2** Tell your friends you have a magic balloon, and offer to show them a trick with it. Inflate the balloon, but not all the way to the end. You need to leave a little space between the real end of the balloon and the false end.

**3** Hold the balloon with one hand on the end of the tail. Tell your friends that this end is too long and pull the tail sharply with your hand.

**4** The false end will come off with a snap. Watch your friends' faces as they try to figure out why the balloon hasn't popped or deflated!

**HANDY HINT**

*Always have a spare balloon ready for this trick in case friends ask you to do it again.*

# There's No Escape!

I don't think the great magician and escape artist Houdini would have much trouble escaping from these handcuffs. Well, at least you don't have to worry about losing the key!

**TIP**
*Don't put these on friends who don't want to wear them – they burst easily if you move around in them.*

**1** Inflate a balloon, leaving only a small uninflated end. Make a small bubble followed by a long bubble. Loop and twist the long bubble to form the first part of the handcuffs. Make sure the loop is big enough for your hand to go through.

**2** Twist the ends of the bubbles together to close the loop. Then prepare another small and long bubble at the other end of the balloon.

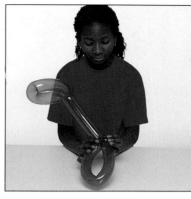

**3** Close the second loop with another loop twist, and you have your own pair of handcuffs. Don't make the loops too tight, or the balloons could pop as you put them on.

**4** Slip the handcuffs on. Now you've got a good excuse: if your hands are locked in these, you can't do any homework!

## ACKNOWLEDGMENTS

*The publishers would like to thank the
following children for modeling for this
book, and their parents and Walnut Tree
Walk Primary School for making it
possible for them to do so:*

Nana Addae
Richard Addae
Leah Bone
William Carabine
Emma Cotton
Lawrence Defraitus
Lee Knight
Barry Lee
Kirsty Lee
Claire McCarthy
Erin McCarthy
Ify Obi
Adenike Odeleye
Fola Oladimeji
Josephina Quayson
Devika Webb

*The author would also like to add
the following:*
Thanks to everyone who has shared
their different balloon ideas over the
years, and especially to the original
inventors, whoever you are. Thanks
also to all makers of chocolate and
orange cookies, which are especially
delicious straight from the fridge!
Apologies to Sophie for having to
do all my typing.